She Brought Color to My Life

Written by Jay Santana

Illustrated by Kim Gatto

To Ava, you brought color and unconditional love to my life.
I am forever thankful to the universe for making me your father.

—JS

To Aimee, Thank you for coloring my world
and being my little girl. I love you infinitely!

—KG

Archway Publishing books may be ordered through booksellers or by contacting:

Archway Publishing
1663 Liberty Drive
Bloomington, IN 47403
www.archwaypublishing.com
844-669-3957

Because of the dynamic nature of the Internet, any web addresses or links contained in this book may have changed since publication and may no longer be valid. The views expressed in this work are solely those of the author and do not necessarily reflect the views of the publisher, and the publisher hereby disclaims any responsibility for them.

Interior Image Credit: Illustrated by © Kim Gatto

ISBN: 978-1-6657-4380-8 (sc)
ISBN: 978-1-6657-4381-5 (hc)
ISBN: 978-1-6657-4293-1 (e)

Print information available on the last page.

Archway Publishing rev. date: 07/27/2023

ARCHWAY
PUBLISHING

She Brought Color to My Life

Written By Jay Santana

Illustrated by Kim Gatto

Once there lived a young man,
full of spirit and fight.

With shoes shined to perfection and his suit pressed nice and tight.

His life was full of grays and browns,
and dark shades of blues.

These were the colors that filled his closet, down to his shiny black shoes.

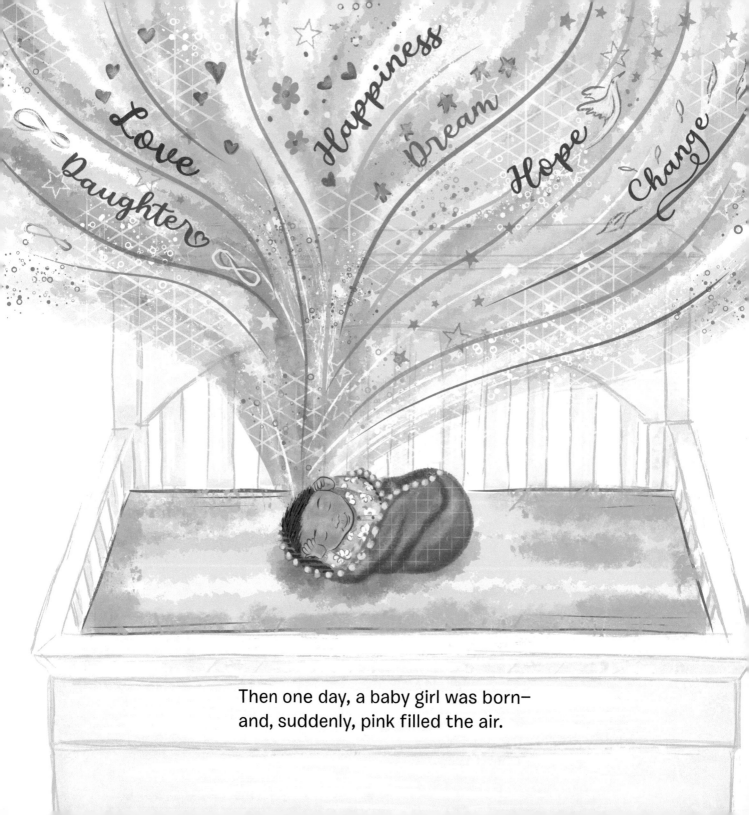

Love

Daughter

Happiness

Dream

Hope

Change

Then one day, a baby girl was born—
and, suddenly, pink filled the air.

Soft browns and purples,
down to the little yellow bow in her hair.

As his baby girl grew,

the colors seemed to multiply with every year.

With every word,

every thought,

every laughter,

and tear.

"Daddy, the sky is blue, and the flowers are pink, yellow, purple, and green."

The colors were everywhere she looked, and in everything she had seen.

The young man, now a father, had changed in ways he never knew he could.

And the colors she brought to his life were in everything he saw, and everywhere he stood.

The colors of the rainbow,
one by one took their place.

Dream —— Dance

Color my world

Love

Love and joy replaced his darkness
and filled the empty space.

A life is incomplete with only grays, browns, and dark shades of blues.

So now, as he stands thankful,
in a pink shirt, purple tie with blue
flowers, and tan leather shoes.

"She brought color to my life," he thinks to himself.
"No other life would I ever choose."

"She brought color . . .

to my life."

This is Jay's first children's book. A published poet, and reformed corporate executive, "She Brought Color to My Life" was written as a poem to his daughter Ava when she was just 3-years old. Life and career ambitions pushed the publication out several years (Ava is now 15-years old). After realizing there is more to life than being at the top of the corporate ladder, Jay decided to step back, spend time with his family and bring his and Ava's story to every father and every daughter. Jay hopes this story brings a smile, sparks a memory, and opens the hearts of every person who flips through its pages. There may be more children's books in Jay's future, but there may not be – perhaps he is the Oscar Wilde or Harper Lee of children's literature.

Kim has been a children's book illustrator and art director for over 20 years, and has drawn MILLIONS of rainbows in her life. But one of the best rainbows of all has been her daughter, Aimee! From the moment she saw her baby girl, she knew her life would be filled with color. Kim hopes this book brings back as many precious memories for readers as it did for her. She lives in Roxbury Township, NJ with her husband Michael, 2 children Derek and Aimee, and 2 cats Milo and Misty, where they continue to color special memories every day. Stop by and say "Hi" to her at www.designsbygatto.com

Printed in the United States
by Baker & Taylor Publisher Services